COUNTRY PROFILES

ETHIOPIA

BY ALICIA Z. KLEPEIS

BLASTOFF!
DISCOVERY

BELLWETHER MEDIA • MINNEAPOLIS, MN

Blastoff! Discovery launches a new mission: reading to learn. Filled with facts and features, each book offers you an exciting new world to explore!

BLASTOFF! UNIVERSE

BLASTOFF! Beginners — GRADE K

BLASTOFF! READERS — GRADES 1-3

BLASTOFF! DISCOVERY — GRADE 4

This edition first published in 2023 by Bellwether Media, Inc.

No part of this publication may be reproduced in whole or in part without written permission of the publisher.
For information regarding permission, write to Bellwether Media, Inc.,
Attention: Permissions Department,
6012 Blue Circle Drive, Minnetonka, MN 55343.

Library of Congress Cataloging-in-Publication Data

Names: Klepeis, Alicia, 1971- author.
Title: Ethiopia / Alicia Z. Klepeis.
Description: Minneapolis : Bellwether Media, 2023. | Series: Blastoff!
    discovery | Includes bibliographical references and index. |
    Audience: Ages 7-13 | Audience: Grades 4-6 | Summary:
    "Engaging images accompany information about Ethiopia.
    The combination of high-interest subject matter and narrative text is
    intended for students in grades 3 through 8"–Provided by publisher.
Identifiers: LCCN 2022016475 (print) | LCCN 2022016476 (ebook)
    | ISBN 9781644877463 (library binding) | ISBN
    9781648347924 (ebook)
Subjects: LCSH: Ethiopia–Juvenile literature. | Ethiopia–Social life and
    customs–Juvenile literature.
Classification: LCC DT373 .F547 2023 (print) | LCC DT373 (ebook)
    | DDC 963–dc23/eng/20220414
LC record available at https://lccn.loc.gov/2022016475
LC ebook record available at https://lccn.loc.gov/2022016476

Editor: Rebecca Sabelko   Designer: Brittany McIntosh

Printed in the United States of America, North Mankato, MN.

TABLE OF CONTENTS

THE DANAKIL DEPRESSION	4
LOCATION	6
LANDSCAPE AND CLIMATE	8
WILDLIFE	10
PEOPLE	12
COMMUNITIES	14
CUSTOMS	16
SCHOOL AND WORK	18
PLAY	20
FOOD	22
CELEBRATIONS	24
TIMELINE	26
ETHIOPIA FACTS	28
GLOSSARY	30
TO LEARN MORE	31
INDEX	32

A tour group arrives at Danakil **Depression**, one of the hottest places on Earth! At its lowest point, the land reaches 410 feet (125 meters) below **sea level**. The smell of rotten eggs from nearby **hot springs** fills the air. The neon yellow water from dried salt looks like nothing else in the world.

OTHER TOP SITES

BLUE NILE FALLS

CHURCH OF SAINT GEORGE

FASIL GHEBBI

NECHISAR NATIONAL PARK

Later, the group hikes up Erta Ale **volcano**. They pass cooled **lava** that looks like crusty black ropes. After a few hours, they reach the **crater** rim. Smoke swirls in the air as they settle into their campsite for the night. Welcome to Ethiopia!

LOCATION

Ethiopia is located in East Africa. It covers 426,373 square miles (1,104,300 square kilometers) of an area called the Horn of Africa. Addis Ababa, the country's capital, is in the center.

Ethiopia is a **landlocked** country. Kenya forms its southern border. South Sudan and Sudan stand to the west. Eritrea is its northern neighbor. Djibouti lies to the northeast. Somalia wraps around Ethiopia's eastern border.

SUDAN

SOUTH SUDAN

RED SEA

ERITREA

A NEW NEIGHBOR

Ethiopia has only been landlocked since 1993. At that time, the area of Eritrea withdrew from Ethiopia. It became a new country. Ethiopia lost its access to the Red Sea.

MEK'ELE

GONDAR

BAHIR DAR

DJIBOUTI

ADDIS ABABA

DIRE DAWA

ETHIOPIA

SOMALIA

KENYA

7

Both highlands and lowlands dominate Ethiopia's landscape. The Blue Nile River enters Ethiopia's Western Lowlands. The land rises into the rugged Western Highlands that include Mount Ras Dejen, the country's highest peak. The Great **Rift** Valley cuts through the center of Ethiopia. Volcanic cones erupt in the valley's northeast. Lakes dot the southwest. The Eastern Highlands rise east of the valley, then gradually slope down into lowlands toward Somalia.

= GREAT RIFT VALLEY
= WESTERN HIGHLANDS

RAS DEJEN
LAKE TANA
BLUE NILE RIVER

LAKE TANA

Located in northwestern Ethiopia, Lake Tana is the country's biggest lake. Despite its size, the lake only reaches 45 feet (14 meters) at its deepest point.

LAKE TANA

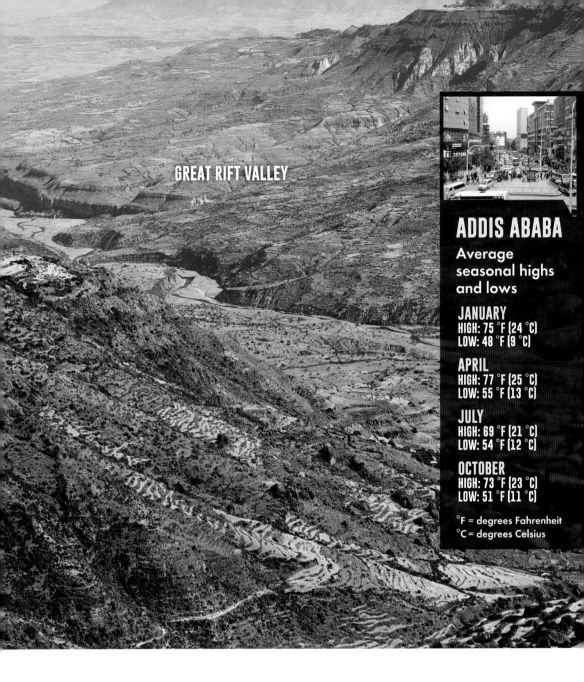

GREAT RIFT VALLEY

ADDIS ABABA

Average
seasonal highs
and lows

JANUARY
HIGH: 75 °F (24 °C)
LOW: 48 °F (9 °C)

APRIL
HIGH: 77 °F (25 °C)
LOW: 55 °F (13 °C)

JULY
HIGH: 69 °F (21 °C)
LOW: 54 °F (12 °C)

OCTOBER
HIGH: 73 °F (23 °C)
LOW: 51 °F (11 °C)

°F = degrees Fahrenheit
°C = degrees Celsius

Ethiopia's climate varies by **elevation**. The highlands
are cooler and wetter than the lowlands. The lowlands can
reach up to 125 degrees Fahrenheit (52 degrees Celsius)!
Rainy seasons occur in March and April and between June
and August.

9

In Ethiopia's lowlands, oryx feed on grasses and thorny shrubs. They look out for hungry wild dogs. Namaqua doves often wander alone in search of seeds. Flocks gather at water holes or where there is a lot of food.

Once **endangered**, geladas now thrive high in the mountains. Groups graze on grasses in highland meadows. Many species of animals in Ethiopia are still endangered. There are very few Simien jackals and mountain nyalas alive today. Many national parks are working to help these endangered animals.

AFRICAN WILD DOG

NAMAQUA DOVE

MOUNTAIN NYALA

YELLOW PANSY BUTTERFLY

BEAUTIFUL BUTTERFLIES

More than 22,000 species of butterflies and moths live in Ethiopia. Colorful types include the yellow pansy butterfly and the marsh commodore moth.

GELADAS

GELADA

Life Span: 14 to 20 years
Red List Status: least concern

gelada range =

LEAST CONCERN	NEAR THREATENED	VULNERABLE	ENDANGERED	CRITICALLY ENDANGERED	EXTINCT IN THE WILD	EXTINCT

Ethiopia is home to more than 113 million people.
Over one in three belong to the Oromo **ethnic** group.
The Amhara make up the second-largest group. Many
smaller ethnic groups make up the rest of the population.
More than 800,000 **refugees** also live in Ethiopia.

Nearly half of Ethiopians practice the Ethiopian Orthodox religion. Many people practice Islam or Protestantism. The country's official national language is Amharic. But some states have other official languages as well.

FAMOUS FACE

Name: Liya Kebede
Birthday: March 1, 1978
Hometown: Addis Ababa, Ethiopia
Famous for: A model, actress, and clothing designer who has served as the World Health Organization's Goodwill Ambassador for Maternal, Newborn and Child Health

SPEAK AMHARIC

Amharic uses script instead of letters. However, Amharic words can be written with the English alphabet so you can read them.

ENGLISH	AMHARIC	HOW TO SAY IT
hello	selam	Seh-Lahm
goodbye (to males)	dehna hun	day-na HOON
goodbye (to females)	denha hunyi	day-na HOON-yee
please (to males)	i'bakih	ih-BAH-keh
please (to females)	i'bakish	ih-BAH-kesh
thank you	ameseginalehu	Ah-meh-seG-nahl-hoo
yes	awo	ah-woh
no	aye	eye

ADDIS ABABA

WOVEN HOMES

The Dorze are master weavers.
They build dome-shaped homes
in the Guge Mountains.
Their homes are made from
bamboo and enset leaves.

Many Ethiopians live in highlands throughout the western half of the country. Over three out of four people live in the countryside. **Rural** homes often have one shared room. Electricity and running water are rare. However, more villages are putting in shared running water. Rural Ethiopians often get around on foot or by horses, mules, or donkeys.

14

Many Ethiopians in the cities live in small apartments. Wealthier people live in bigger homes. Electricity is available in most **urban** areas. People often travel by bus or taxi. A metro system opened in 2015.

ADDIS ABABA

Ethiopia has a rich musical history. The *tsenatsil* is a kind of rattle used in **traditional** Ethiopian music. The *begena* is a stringed instrument known for its buzzing sound. Musicians often play it during religious ceremonies. Painters have created richly colored works for centuries. Many trained at the Alle School of Fine Art and Design in Addis Ababa.

WOMEN PLAYING *BEGENAS*

WOMEN WEARING
HIJABS

PHOTOGRAPHY IN ETHIOPIA

Photography is becoming a popular art form in Ethiopia. Eyerusalem Jiregna is an Ethiopian photographer whose work is shown around the globe!

In urban areas, Ethiopians commonly wear Western-style clothing. Muslim women usually wear long, loose-fitting dresses called *abayas*. They cover their hair with *hijabs*, or headscarves. Different ethnic groups often have their own styles of dress.

Children in Ethiopia begin primary school at age 7. They are required to attend school for eight years. But many children leave school early to work. Students learn in the main language of their area until around fifth grade. Secondary school classes are taught in English. Students must pass exams to study at a university.

Over 7 out of 10 Ethiopians are farmers. They grow maize, wheat, sweet potatoes, and sugarcane. Other people have **service jobs**. The **tourism** industry employs workers in hotels, in national parks, and at many historical sites. Factories make **textiles**, leather goods, and processed foods.

TEXTILE MARKET

BIRTHPLACE OF COFFEE

The coffee plant is from Ethiopia. The country is Africa's biggest coffee producer. The sale of coffee earns a lot of money for the nation.

COFFEE FARMER

SOCCER

Soccer is the most popular sport in Ethiopia. Loza Abera, known as the Goal Queen, has helped to advance women's soccer in Ethiopia in recent years. Many Ethiopians take part in track and field. Ethiopian runners have won many long-distance races around the globe.

TRACK AND FIELD

In cities, teenagers often meet friends at cafes or restaurants. Rural teenagers gather at community events and markets. Ethiopians often get together to play games such as chess or cards. It is common for children to make their own toys rather than buy them.

MARKET

CLAY POT

Ethiopians have a rich tradition of pottery making. There are clay pots for cooking, serving coffee, and more! Your pot will not be safe to use for cooking or serving food.

What You Need:
- blank paper
- pencil
- air-dry clay
- butter knife (optional)
- acrylic or tempera paints (optional)

What You Do:
1. Look in books or online to find examples of clay pots from Ethiopia.
2. Sketch a design for your pot on your piece of paper.
3. Use your sketch to guide you as you use your hands to form a pot from your clay. If you decide to make a design on your pot, use your butter knife to lightly mark the clay's surface. You do not want to cut all the way through the clay.
4. After the clay dries completely, you can paint it if you wish. Let the paint dry completely.
5. Place your pot someplace special to display it.

A SIP OF SPRISS

Many juice houses in Addis Ababa serve spriss. This drink includes three layers of different fruit juices. Popular flavors include mango, pineapple, and avocado.

MAKING *INJERA*

Most Ethiopian meals include a spongy bread called *injera*. People use this bread to eat many dishes. One example is injera paired with *beyainatu*. This variety of vegetables, lentils, and potatoes is served in little piles. Another example is the curry dish called *wot*, made with chicken, beef, or goat.

Ethiopians add a spice mix called *berbere* to a lot of meals. It can contain cinnamon, chili powder, ginger, and cardamom. A special dish in northern Ethiopia is *ti'hilo*. Eaters use carved sticks to dip barley balls into a hot sauce made of flour and **pulses**.

BEYAINATU

TI'HILO

HIMBASHA

Make a teatime snack or late breakfast of this flatbread. Have an adult help you make it.

Ingredients:
1/2 packet (or 1 teaspoon) dry yeast
1 cup lukewarm water
2 tablespoons sugar
2 cups flour, plus extra for rolling
1/2 teaspoon salt
1 teaspoon black sesame seeds
1 teaspoon ground cardamom
3 tablespoons vegetable oil, plus extra for greasing

Steps:
1. Pour yeast into 1 cup of lukewarm water. Stir in the sugar and put in a warm place for 10 minutes or until it bubbles.

2. In a large bowl, mix the flour, salt, sesame seeds, and cardamom. Mix the yeast mixture and oil into the dry ingredients.

3. Knead the dough on a lightly floured surface until it is smooth.

4. Place the kneaded dough into a lightly greased bowl and cover it with plastic wrap. Put the bowl in a warm place for an hour.

5. Preheat your oven to 350 degrees Fahrenheit (177 degrees Celsius). Then, roll the dough into a large circle. Place this into a 12-inch greased pan.

6. Brush the dough lightly with oil. Bake for about 20 minutes until the bread is golden. Serve with melted butter when it has cooled. Enjoy!

ENKUTATASH

TIME TRAVELERS

Ethiopia's calendar has 13 months. It is also in a different year than most of the world. While most countries were in September of 2022, Ethiopia marked the start of 2015!

Ethiopia uses its own unique calendar. People celebrate New Year's, known as *Enkutatash*, in September. Families often give gifts to children during this time. People also have a traditional meal and pick seasonal yellow flowers.

Many Ethiopian holidays are religious. In late September, Christians celebrate *Meskel*. It marks the discovery of the cross on which people believe Jesus Christ died. People light bonfires as part of the celebration. They also sing and dance. Muslims pray, feast, and give to the poor each year during *Eid al-Fitr*. This holiday ends a month-long period of **fasting** called Ramadan. Throughout the year, Ethiopians celebrate their traditions and people!

MESKEL

1889
Addis Ababa becomes the country's capital city

4TH CENTURY
Christianity becomes the official religion of Ethiopia

1941
Ethiopian and British troops defeat the Italians and Haile Selassie returns to power

1935–1936
Italian troops invade and claim Ethiopia, and the Ethiopian emperor, Haile Selassie, is forced out of the country

13TH CENTURY
The 11 rock churches at Lalibela are built as a site for religious journeys for Ethiopian Christians

1984–1985
Food shortages affect millions of Ethiopians

1994
A new constitution divides Ethiopia into regions based on ethnic groups

1974
A group of military officers known as the Derg come into power, beginning a period of conflict among the nation's people

1993
The province of Eritrea breaks away from Ethiopia, taking away Ethiopia's access to the Red Sea

2018
Sahle-Work Zewde is elected Ethiopia's first woman president

Official Name: Federal Democratic Republic of Ethiopia

Flag of Ethiopia: The flag of Ethiopia has three horizontal stripes. The top one is green, which represents hope and the country's natural resources. The center stripe is yellow and stands for justice and harmony. The bottom stripe is red as a symbol of the sacrifices Ethiopians made for their nation. In the center of the flag is a blue circle. Blue represents peace. The yellow star in the middle of the circle stands for equality and unity of Ethiopians.

Area: 426,373 square miles
(1,104,300 square kilometers)

Capital City: Addis Ababa

Important Cities: Dire Dawa, Mek'ele, Gondar, Bahir Dar

Population:
113,656,596 (2022 est.)

WHERE PEOPLE LIVE

COUNTRYSIDE
77.3%

CITY
22.7%